TO BE DISRESPECTED JUST FOR OCCUPYING SPACE

DENISE JONES

Copyright © 2024 by Denise Jones

Paperback: 978-1-961438-03-3
eBook: 978-1-961438-04-0
Library of Congress Control Number: 2023909018

All rights reserved. No part of this publication may be reproduced, distributed, or transmitted in any form or by any electronic or mechanical means, without the prior written permission of the publisher, except in the case of brief quotations embodied in critical reviews and certain other noncommercial uses permitted by copyright law.

Ordering Information:

Prime Seven Media
518 Landmann St.
Tomah City, WI 54660

Printed in the United States of America

Table of Contents

Prologue 1

Chapter 1: Little Girl Lost 3

Chapter 2: Finding my way back 45

Chapter 3: Leftovers 97

PROLOGUE

This book is for healing and moving forward in a positive way. The entries of a little girl lost is my life, what I went through as a little girl.

It took me over 20 years to begin to look in the mirror and find a way back. The rape I experienced at 11 years old changed the path of my life. I struggled for years to find someone that I could trust. My trust chip was destroyed. Never came back. I'm 77 and my health is not great.

I need to give abused girls and women direction and courage to find love and respect for themselves. Self-love is the first thing necessary to have a positive life.

I experienced these stories, these horrific things at an early age. I hope this book is an eye-opener for abused girls to stop and find something good about themselves. Our healing begins with ourselves.

I looked in the mirror one day and finally saw something good and beautiful about me. Stay positive and strong. God Bless.

LITTLE GIRL LOST

This story is about the devastation of growing up without love and acceptance. Being abused raped and sodomized. Treated like I was a being tolerated more than appreciated for who I was.

Writing the book is closure for me and the hope of being able to save some young girl from herself. I have been though a lot. My patience with bullshit is zero. I absolutely hate liars, phonies and users.

I have developed into a 77-year-old woman who has no filter. If the truth is known most people can't understand who I am or what I'm about. Living my life now is difficult. Poor health. Chronic pain. Isolated from relationships.

Even to this day. My ability to trust has been damaged. I actually prefer to be alone. I wish that I could feel the warmth of love from someone other than my pets. I love the few people that I have let in my life.

I love them dearly, not being sure if they will desert me. Sadly, to this day it is still hard for me to believe that anyone will want to be close to me once they get to know me. How sad, huh. Yeah. I'm who I am and have no interest in changing for anyone. That is the truth.

Cut and dry. I live with 5 beautiful little cats, lol one little dog and six birds. We are ok. We love each other and are ok left alone. Animals can teach us humans a lot about compassion and emotional honesty. I am living in Canada now. I prefer Los Angeles, that's right. I spent many years there. My mentality is more American.

I'm too straight out the box for a lot of Canadians. I don't waste time with words and useless emotions. It's all or nothing. I've been trapped in poverty most of my life. Struggling to survive, it's not even about the money. Sure, it's a necessity to have a place to live, food, health care. A little nest egg for emergencies. But having the actual ambition of becoming rich? Never had it. We can't get to heaven in a Cadillac.

Having my special gift of intense intuition all my life has also saved me many times from myself and people that wanted to hurt me.

It's never been about material things. Sure, I like pleasant things, don't misunderstand me. But they don't come first.

What is the sad reality of my life? I know that there are many people that know what I'm talking about and can understand the meaning of leftovers.

I struggle everyday with the lack of interest in letting people in to penetrate my protective barrier that has been developed over the years.

Having an identity problem from being adopted and never really knowing my true roots somewhat changed upon finding my beautiful brothers. That has been the best positive experience about being accepted for myself.

People come into our lives for the purpose of becoming aware of who we really are and loving who we are. Time for everything.

Faded Memories

One time when my mother took her nap in the afternoon. I hid under the table; I still can't figure out why I was hiding. So weird some of the things I do remember. What was I afraid of?? Like I said. I don't remember any happy times, none. That's deep.

I had this uncle that was shell shocked in WW1. He used to visit us at the weekends. We used to have this long walk thru closet from his room to mine.

I still don't remember whether he was in my room or not. Whether it was reality, or it was a nightmare, this memory I have of him.

He definitely was a war leftover and weird as hell. I was very afraid of him.

When I used to get punished for about everything I did, I would have to go to the basement. I was forced to run up and down the stairs a whole bunch of times, and write "I must not do this; I must not do that". I remember sitting on the top of the basement stairs being scared shitless.???? Why??? I don't have any memory of my sister doing this.

My adopted parents had a real daughter. We weren't close. She was my mom's favorite. My dad used to stick up for me a lot. But he couldn't do much because my mother was in charge. He was hen pecked big time.

I got very depressed the couple times I went home to visit. It had to be the flash backs getting to me.

The story of my assault at age 11 is that I was sodomized and raped by an older guy 17 year old who worked for my dad. This incident ruined my life, my journey was completely shattered after that.

He picked me up from the skating rink one chilly winter night. He worked for my dad doing winter chores and farming and ate dinner with us many times. He asked if I wanted a ride home. I trusted him.

It was a tiny town In Manitoba in the dead of winter. He took me out of town, stopped the car. Grabbed me by my hair and pulled me down. Punched me in the stomach, knocked the air out of me.

He raped and sodomized me. Tore me apart, hurt me very badly. He told me he was going to kill me. Then said if you don't tell anyone. I might let you live.

He left me out on the country road, a mile out of town. It was freezing and dark. I was so afraid, scared shitless, bleeding, crying. Blood running down my leg. I almost froze getting home.

I was never the same . I turned into an incredibly angry, self-abusive young lady. Mad as hell.

I was wild after that, nobody deserves this indignity to their body, to their soul. To this day I suffer because if it. I've blocked most of it. The pain, comparable to giving birth. I was only 11 years old!

The rape took something away from me that I can never get back. Gone forever was my youthful innocence. I was a child 11 years old. Perhaps, if I was older, it might have been a bit easier to get over.

But I was not just a little girl, I was a virgin. Anyway, the bastard is dead now. Good!!! Something fell on him. Ha-ha looks good on him. I don't remember the actual event, but I do remember losing something. Something vital to form attachments to people.

The ability to trust, to bond is actually gone. It was destroyed by the rape and other terrible stuff I endured in my childhood and later years. Imagine having to turn tricks with hundreds of old men at 16 years old. This was my lovely karma that the universe had dished out for me from the very beginning.

Yes, I believe in karma, and the bitch is karma that comes from other lifetimes. Life is not fair. Far from it. I'm not just crying about my own shitty experiences. What about all the innocent children, getting tortured, murdered, raped. Starving to death. For what damn reason I'll never understand. This is why karma is definitely a reality. I'm not a Christian nor would I ever set foot in another church. But I love our Creator God. And I do believe in the laws of Karma. Cause and Effect. It is so true.

I was not the only one he had raped. Very , very tragic

I was situated in Los Angeles back in the 70's. South Central LA, Compton. Tough areas, gang bangers. A militant hostile environment.

I used to go to this bar in Compton. I was the only woman in there with teeth lol. I kept my little .22 in my purse. The women gave me a tough time sometimes but I had a good relationship with most of the ghetto women. Some, though, women can be real bitches.

I found that out when I was still in diapers. I had a man, married man. Loved him, we were so close. I used to dance in a bar. A Go Go girl, trying to survive. He used to hang out there to cheer me on. I was a good dancer and had a body that would cause car accidents.

I had my daughters to take care of and they were little girls at the time. I made my living from the streets. It was freaking hard to survive. There were times I would get so high on weed almost fell off the stage. Lol.

When I first got to LA I stayed with my girlfriend's mother. She was a piece of work. I was wild picking up men. A different one every night. Jumbo's Clown Room on

As I enter this ancient place, where you and I don't belong. I get this feeling there all the time, that something is going down wrong. Make no mistake and you will find everything you need down here.

The herb houses are full of roots and things. With their promise of a cure. The dying go there as a last resort. Their money they will take for sure. The narrow streets are jammed tight and it's hard to get by the people in front of me.

The vegetable stands are full, ready for picking. As the police go by, they will be gone in the blink of an eye. The Chinese greens are there for sale. Everyone wants some of them. The fish is out there stinking in the hot sun shining down. You see life is so simple in old' China Town. Day after day it begins again with the familiar sights and sounds. Constantly, same time same place. Nothing changes from day to day. If you mess up in old' China Town, The Tong men are going to get you. There is no need to call the police. Your life is going to be through. A judge, jury, and executioner will be there waiting for you.

The Kung Fu studio has a secret door to the gambling house on the next floor where the money flows like water. The store front fakes you out. No hint of what's going on within. Money is changed to yen. Enough to buy a pie in the sky. More than you and I could ever spend.

The old whore house is hidden behind the acupuncture sign. The alley is how you get in. The men are discreet disappearing in the streets. And you don't see them again. Make no mistake, what goes on there is more than therapeutic.

The old men sneak in the back door of the whore house down the street. They are so cheap that their asses squeak. There are no rich whores down here. They will do anything, I guarantee you, for the money they will send for that family back home, for that haunting memory of that long boat ride will never be silenced again. The roaches jump up and fly in old' China Town. The basements are moldy and bare.

You can be sure that anything is going on there. The girls are so cute in their birthday suits. Exchanging sex for money.

They are all the same playing their games. So desperate it's a shame. That's how the shit goes down in old' China Town. Make no mistake about it.

The money, there is millions and more which none of it we'll get. So, it's all so clear that money stays here. That is guaranteed.

The old men sit around in their yards. Playing their card games all day. Talking that talk, walking that walk. And, in old' China Town they'll stay.

Second time Around

It was your claim to fame. From the backside of the mirror. There are cobwebs in this memory, and the dust has become sticky. The looking glass has shattered, fallen inside of itself. Like a dream the vision fades, and it's ghost-like quality is strong. Reality of many moons ago. Old mansions in the hills. There is a presence of the lives, from centuries so long ago. I went once again to the vision I could see, looking back at me. The old life I knew in ancient times.

It was a cool evening in late September. I started out on one of my dangerous adventures. I'm a heroin addict and could care less about anything except getting high. It was 1960, I was almost 16 years old. I stopped off at the Chinese hotel on the corner of a busy street in old Chinatown. I slowly walked in knowing full well I had to fuck and suck at least 10 nasty old men. I was so immune to the full process that I felt nothing, not even disgust.

I stopped off at the first room on the ground floor old Mister Chang. He was one of the many smelly bastards that I had to put up with. He actually wasn't so bad as some of them. He always offered me food. Rotten fruit and moldy meat. He meant well but I actually don't think his nose worked.

He was one of my younger clients, the ripe age of 81. I wondered why I was getting turned off from sex lol. How ironic. He had one of those little bitty dicks and a cheesy set of balls. Ugg. It was always the first 2-3 clients that were the most revolting. It was because I wasn't high yet, so the reality of the whole situation got to me sometimes. I spent 1/2 hr. with Mr. Stinky Chang.

He gave me 6 dollars for an uncovered BJ and sex . My first experience with sex was a forceful rape and sodomy. Then I went on to get gang banged and now this. Old nasty men. I was numb actually. I finished with Mr. Chang and went on to the third floor. I had to use the bathroom.

They had one at the end of each floor. Nasty as hell. Unbelievable 20 old men using the same bathroom ● After stepping over the disgusting mess on the floor, I went to Mr. Wong's room.

He took a bath once a year whether he needed it or not ● I was there 25 minutes. He gave me 5 bucks. ● I left the room, ran down the hall, the rickety stairs. Outside it was getting dark now. I walked four blocks to the dope house, took my 5 dollars and got a hit of heroin.

I sat down on a wobbly chair, took out my outfit. I shot it all within 15 minutes. All of a sudden, I had to run to the bathroom and throw up. I was always nauseated for a few minutes. Threw up and felt better. So now I went back and sat down, shot the shit for a while. I got up and left.

It was dark now. I stopped off at the greasy spoon and tried to eat something. Fell asleep. Nodded off in my food. Head went right in my food. So now I wanted to get high again it was starting to wear off. John the waiter kicked me out.

He told me, "you sleep in food, no good" . Now I had to get a trick on the street. It was dark. Scary shit. Jumping in those fricking cars. I was really surprised that I have survived those mean streets. I jumped in with this harmless looking old white man. Grey hair, nice car yeah right!! The bastard took me out of town.

On the outskirts he looked at me with these cold eyes and told me that this was the day I was going to die. ● ● ● . Shit I was scared but I wasn't about to let the bastard know. l wasn't going to beg because it was a waste of time. He stopped the car and slapped the shit out of me. No one around for miles, one of those country roads. I knew this was going to be an all-out fight for my life.

He tried to strangle me; I fought like hell. I somehow got the door open. I poked the bastard in his eyes, dug him good. I started running, my drawers were wet. I had pissed myself, I was so scared. I ran like crazy in those dark woods, my heart was beating so fast I couldn't breathe. I heard him behind me, but luckily, he fell down. I took that opportunity to hide behind a bush.

I heard him near me, but it was so dark, he passed by me and then started back to the car. The sick fucker drove off. I was so scared, too scared to move. Stayed there all night in those dark woods. Crying and shivering. The morning seemed like a million light years away. Finally, it started to get light. I was so tired; I didn't know what to do. I knew I was at least 20 miles out of the city.

I started walking down the country road, I was extremely nervous and paranoid. This farmer pulled up behind me and I started yelling. He stopped and gave me a ride back to the city. Nice guy. I couldn't believe it. I caught the bus back to my temporary home.

I was living with this old Pilipino man. He had to be at least 85. He was a kind old man. He was gone when I got there, I just collapsed. I was starting to get sick. I had a 75- dollar day heroin habit. That was a lot of money in 1961. This was just one day.

Let me quit tripping for now. I just realized something about myself lately. I really have been somewhat of a recluse. Having a lot of people around me drives me nuts.

I've been alone so much I'm used to it now. I've got a lot of anger inside of me especially when it comes to dealing with certain areas of my life that I can't change. You have that old saying if you can't fix it don't force it.

I'm also finding out that nowadays people don't really face reality like they should. They are hiding behind big, beautiful houses, cars, clothes. People have a problem, that when it is not convenient then don't waste time.

Nobody has time for sacrificing any of themselves for other people. Sure, you have the volunteers who really are there for the purple heart more than anything else. I don't remember one day when I felt happy within myself.

Other things made me happy, but to find happiness within myself, no it's just not there. I'm trying to find a reason for this. I'll go back to the times that I really can't remember. I was born in a hospital in a cold assed city in a situation where I was not really wanted. I still don't understand how anyone could have given away a little baby as cute as I was. Lol. But shit happens and we live, don't we? I was raised in an army camp situation. No room for self-discovery.

I did what I was told or got my ass tore up by my adopted mother. She was a very hard-core woman when she was young. She had so much self-control and even now in her 80's she still does. I really can't say what happened to me under twelve years old because I can barely remember anything.

That is so sad that I have such a terrible memory of my past. It's the drugs I took. My long-term memory is shot. I can remember a couple instances when I was humiliated. I was standing at the front of the class and pissed my pants.

What an embarrassment. I remember getting in trouble fighting with one of the girls I grew up with. I hit the bitch in the head with a skate guard, she if course ran home and told her mother. What a little bitch, lol. I got beat up. I always remember being alone in my own little world.

It's a very lonely journey to go through life alone. Never being able to hang onto love, friends, family. My trust in humanity has been shattered, and have never been able to get it back to 100%.

I have realized over the years I have been able to let a few people in. I never get over the feeling of waiting for the knife in my back, or the very hurtful betrayal of my trust.

These stories are raw and deep. If you have ever gotten to the point in your life that you can relate to my stories then maybe this book is the book that will help save you. Help you find yourself.

I'm an old lady been to hell and back. Physically, emotionally, and spiritually. I know because of the abuse, I had to self-destruct to be able to hit rock bottom.

The place where there was no more existence at all. I couldn't exist anymore. I had to change directions, dig deep in my soul and find myself under a pile of regrets and mistakes.

Years went by after my rape before I could pull myself together. This horrible monster changed the course of my life. It took over 20 years to find a reason to move on.

The poor girls and women that have been sexually abused have a piece of their soul gone. It's true. There is a terrible price to pay for sexual abuse. It's like a dagger in the pit if your soul. It really amazes me that people can think girls can't remember who attacked them.

You will never forget it. Certain men and boys have a history of this horrific behavior. It's never just once.

This journey of always looking for love and acceptance has never ended to this day.

I still feel in my soul that I can't let anyone in. It's a very lonely journey to go through life alone. Never being able to hang onto love, friends. My trust in humanity has been shattered.

AFRICA

What a shock to realize I was there without a return trip ticket!! My husband was an asshole and a control freak. Since I'm not the kind of woman that is able to take any man trying to control me, and l soon realized I was at his mercy.

I lived across the street from a noisy mosque. Noisy as hell early in the morning. It was a revelation to me to acknowledge the cultural differences, and the scary reality of my situation.

My husband could have murdered my ass, and nobody would have known. He wanted four wives and of course l told him over my dead body. I told him I wanted to go back to the states but I didn't have any money for my ticket.

I was dependent on him for everything. His family was rich, dad was a lawyer. We lived in a house with bars on every window and door.

We lived next to the very scary Lagos ghetto where naked children lived in straw huts. I quickly learned how primitive Lagos was in 1982. No phones in most homes except for the rich. We had to go to the international phone center. Very noisy.

We had an argument one day and I ran away. I was white, lol not good. Being native and French didn't matter. There are only two races there white or black it's really obvious.

I have the mentality of a black American woman and my mouth and attitude got me in trouble. It was hard for me to keep my opinions to myself. I lived with him and his brother and his wife. She was a real bitch. Always picking on me.

We had no bathtub or shower. Lol just had to take Cowboys with freezing water. No toilet paper, wiping your butt with leaves lol. I was not impressed. His sister was ok with me. She lived in England for a while and the neighbors were cool with me.

The woman would sit on the street and sell cigarettes one at a time. Never seen such big butts in all my life lol. My neighbor had a butt you could put a chair on. I would say damn you got a big butt and she would crack up laughing. She actually had a shower in her house.

I took a cab ride when I ran away. Almost got in trouble. Had to slap the shit out of him and had to jump out of a moving cab. Shit.

It was an extremely dangerous place. He took me to the Lagos museum. The president's car had 200 bullet holes in it. He showed me this big black pot told me this is where they boiled the poor white people and ate them lol.

I told him fuck you and we would laugh like hell. He really was a spoiled asshole his family sent him to Los Angeles to go to school. that's how I met him.

He was a male exotic dancer and he was looking good lol. I love black American men only because of the whole mentality of America. I need the humor, the understanding.

LA and RAY

Ray and I packed up the kids and headed for LA. They were young. Ray was a wannabe pimp, he couldn't pimp his way out a wet paper bag, he was too soft. We were leaving Seattle.

My best girlfriend lives in LA now. I was really excited about moving there. We survived the trip and moved in with Jackie's mother. She was a real piece of work. Started dancing as a Go-Go dancer. Was high, smoking plenty of weed.

Ray went his own way and we would spend time together once in a while. Not long after we got there, he died from Leukemia. He got really sick. It was incredibly sad and I still miss him. We were remarkably close. Got my girls in school. We got our own place, had to get government assistance. Danced under the table. Had lots of fun. We were extremely poor, went out a lot, was a party animal.

Danced at Jumbo's clown room. Went topless lol. Got plenty of tips. Met a couple of girlfriends. We are friends to this day.

They both lived in the ghetto. I used to hangout and go to the clubs. Met lots of guys lol. I was pretty wild back then.

Ghetto

We all sleep in the back rooms, far away from the street. Because baby, when those bullets fly. I'm sure there's one you'll eat.

The dog's barking so loud tonight, I wonder who's out there. But one thing is for sure, he'll get a damn good scare. The dog is guarding the house, waiting for his reward. The bone that he wants, I'm sure I can't afford.

This feels like I'm in prison, with at these all these bars around me. I can't take any chances tonight. It's mother's day and the money's right. The zombies and the strawberries are in heat.

Roaming the streets, humping the curbs for their old winter feast. Five dollars will take you to the moon, on a one-way trip. AIDS is here, better double bag it and be sure to you use someone else's dick.Just in case you play Russian roulette with a whore. Shit baby I can't understand why you got to go down so hard, and you better be catching a bus before dark, or you'll be hitching ride. No buses go where the ghost busters' slide.

The freaks run wild in the streets. The cluck heads are running it down, to anyone they will meet. The cars drive by as

I look around. Never being sure who's in them. You'll be nervous you can bet on that. Jumping out of your skin.

There's always a surprise, like a snake in the grass. Waiting to strike as you pass. So be discreet, on the way to the corner, down the street. At the liquor store you'll be sure to meet the old winos hanging out there.

It's hard to relax in a world of nightmares, one mistake and baby you're through. You'll get your ass smoked and it ain't no joke. But you had shit for brains, couldn't stay home. So, down to the corner you went.

Reaching your prime ain't worth a dime. And what do you do when they're tired of you and come looking for your ass again. The veteran on the street. His mind long gone, shooting his gun like he's still in Vietnam, howling at the moon in broad daylight. So, it's better to stay home in the backroom, ready to shoot the first thing that moves. Like a junk yard dog, you fit in, and Fort Knox is your home again. Searching the streets.

The helicopters are flying, neighborhood children are dying. When the sun goes down, it's like a ghost town. Ashes to ashes. Dust to dust.

In reality who can you trust? You can't be friendly anymore, not on the bus. Went and sat near the back door. Might as well have a sign on me, rob me for sure. so, baby you think you're all that, come to LA 204818 where I'm from you won't last a day.

They'll chew you up and spit you out. And right on the curb you'll stay. So be smart and bypass the ghetto. Life is rough, and the streets are tough aren't nothing for you out today.

I lived in the Los Angeles ghetto for 25 years. Compton 4 years. People treated me like a Latino. I used to strut my stuff on the street with a long blond wig on lol, oh, that was not cool.

I would get attacked by bitches all the time. Bullets flying on Western + Normandie and 59th. Normandie and 75th. Living on the edge of violence and uncertainty. I danced in a ghetto bar with my friend.

We used to go out to clubs. Hang out both of us carrying guns in our purses 1980 - 81 wild west. I knew all the bangers. They drive around in their beat up cars five or six at a time. We were sitting at home on 59th and Normandy, bullets flying through the front door. I was there at the heart of the Watts riot.

Ghost stories of ghetto life, all true. Nobody would be able to stand the desperation and hopelessness of a ghetto life. The stories are all true. I was there experienced it lived it.

I had a married man. yeah, I know. But I loved him. And he loved me. He used to hang out at the bar where I danced. He was extremely sweet. we were remarkably close. I had a body that would cause a car accident lol.

The Mean

Having been a heroin addict at 15, it is a miracle I even survived. The streets were unbelievably life changing.

I survived 8 years in the streets and in the whore houses. I would have done anything to get high. I was an impossible heroin addict at 16.

I would do anything to get high. ● I had sex with over 1000 grown men before my 18th birthday. No self-respect. No value of myself as a human being.

I was nobody to myself and everyone else. I was pimped and beat up for several years. Finally, I got tired of that Old China Town hotels were so dingy and dark.

The old Chinese men were spending time together in the halls. I would go there, go from room to room. Stay a couple of hours then leave.

I had a pimp back in those days, and a couple more before I was through. He wasn't too bad but didn't mind taking my money.

After work I would go to this club owned by this old man I stayed with. Big Daddy's club. Yeah. I stayed there all night.

Hung out with these famous singers back in the day. Etta James, James Brown. They would come to Vancouver to his club.

I had fun there, listening to that good music. Actually, me and Jesse stayed at his house. He got many famous black entertainers.

I would spend time together there all night after work. My life was terribly busy with drugs and partying. Underage, under the table, which was my life.

During the day and until midnight I did tricks. This hotel was full of old men. Nasty old' men. In Chinatown. Never ever took baths.

Shit I must have had sex with every last one of them. 200 or more!!! I was getting very mad at life and ended up in jail for a year.

The Reality Check 1998 Toronto

Well life turned out to be different these days. I just found out 2 weeks ago I got Hep C. I didn't really realize the entire situation, but I am starting to now. To be brutally honest I'm scared shitless about my future. It is a very unpredictable disease. Different outcomes. Eventually 80% of all cases start showing symptoms. I guess there is a good chance I could have a fatal disease. I can't believe I'm writing this shit, but this is the way I feel. Have you ever stopped for a minute and thought about the consequences? Yeah. This is a very hard lesson to learn. The danger of choices. We all have to do what we have to do, right? Whatever it takes to try to survive. That's what it's all about. Looking back now, I can see it's been one hard struggle for me to achieve any kind of happiness. The few times I thought I was doing the right thing I wasn't even then. Years ago, I used to just live for the day never thinking about tomorrow. Maybe even back then I was fine, at least I thought I was. Turned into the aspect of reality, don't count your chickens before they hatch. I still have the same attitude about life, one day at a time. Maybe that's one of the major reasons that I never troubled myself too much to acquire any significant amount of money. I could never see much sense in dreaming about a future, a future to me was like a privilege. Yeah, it's a privilege to get old. Don't you think? Getting older damn.!!! I'm 50 years old now. What a trip. I can't believe I'm 50. Shit!! It took a lot of years to figure out the downside of life. I was a party girl. Big time. I loved to party. I partied with the best, stayed up all night, stayed awake for days. Sleep what??? I never had time to sleep.

Haunted Past

I went to parties. Got drunk. Had sex with many guys. My self-esteem got even worse. My reputation got terrible.

Growing up in Manitoba during the 50's was bad enough. Adopted kids were not treated well. This is my low self-esteem escalated to such a dangerous and harmful level.

At 14-15 went to Winnipeg to work for a Jewish family and started hairdressing school. Never finished school, never finished grade 10. I just really gave up; I didn't even realize. I went to school and started going wrong very quickly.

Started going to parties. Dirty Dot's party house. It was a very wild time. Met a married man, thought I was in love. But of course, I lost because I couldn't believe anyone could love me.

It was my first experience that I thought love was all about. The degrading things I did and the way I carried myself. I had no self-respect. And of course, none for anyone else.

I lasted less than 6 months and met some guy and took off for Vancouver. I had no love for myself and my value of who I was didn't exist. I was a nobody and didn't stand a chance.

Some minds can't accept a lost challenge of regret and won't continue on in the rat race of existence. Who are you to say you care??? Huh!! Oh, my that is so touching to who's ears.

The ears of the past. Take off your mask honey. The curtain fell on you many moons ago. Yes indeed!! It really surprises the aware mind that any one fragment of life could possible survive all those self-made tortures.

To inflict pain on your own unique mind. What a waste. The plot was only to conquer and after the challenge there was nothing left. Is that the extent of your game? Or does your mind run deeper than the impression it gives?

The accused is very unaware of the reasons for doing things. How could you forget the lines you knew so well? After all this was your play, your performance. It was a who's show. One monkey don't stop the show. Or does it.

The Past Haunts

The thing that hurts the most is that although I'm not a needy person when I needed a friend the most, I had none. My friend in LA was useless.

She will not and cannot help me in my desperate struggle. I am terribly upset lately. Because of the fact that I have trust issues it is exceedingly difficult for me to reach out.

I realize now the very few that I have allowed to get close to me, including my own daughters, have disappointed me.

They refuse to even try to understand. It makes me feel the terrible impact of being alone when there is no one to reach out to.

My friend has totally turned away from me. She has always been selfish and shallow.

She refuses to acknowledge the fact that she is not helping me cope with my many problems 99% of my problems are physical, the rest is money.

Typical normal problems. I have health issues and once in a while I need to talk about how frustrating it is to have complicated illnesses.

Anyway, I hate to reach out to anyone for anything. I seem to always get dumped on.

Issue of Lack of Trust

Trust is the most important thing in any relationship. Starting with honesty. When I realized that a large part of my life has been wasted. I was never able to finish anything I started. It's like I don't have the joy of life to even try. I try for my pets, yeah you are damn right. It's depressing and sad. The old lady was so depressed. Trying to survive financially. The thing about survival is that once you really understand that you are alone it becomes crystal clear what you have to do. I have no friends. I don't feel close to anyone right now, So don't trust anyone at all. I will go to the end of my life with this problem. Not being able to trust. Being given away at birth contributed to this. Killed it for me. The trust of a mother. She dumped me twice. I wish I had never searched for her. It seems like such a wasted effort. Very sad. When I met her, I didn't feel anything. No emotion. I guess when I think about it, it makes sense. Some adopted kids are really lucky to have a successful reconnection with their families. I feel sorry for her being in a relationship with a controlling man. It was because of him that she backed off. The bastard!! Bitter huh? Damn Skippy I am. This book is not for pussies. If you can't stand the harsh reality of what never was and never will be. These are the cold harsh facts of the life of the little girl lost. Me, that's right. I'm ok now, won't take a second of shit off anyone.

Rubber Band Man

To be so stretched out of shape, losing strength and power. Pulled in so many directions. Never having a chance to recover. Worn thin by being used. Being broken from abuse. The Rubber Band man, getting disrespected just for occupying space. With such a resilient spirit. With your tragic yesterday. How can you escape? The victim of your fate. Being unique in your pain, yours is different. A man different from the rest, with a haunted past. To be disrespected just for occupying space. Just for your existence you are tormented. Never being accepted as a man. No acknowledgement as a human being. When will they realize the damage, they've done? Just like Humpy Dumpty, you will never be the same again. Your humility runs deep, too deep to recover. Having given up so much, just to survive. In a world of rejection, a world of disrespect. As a man of soul. You bounce back. The Rubber Band Man. Being stretched out of shape. Alone in his fate. Different from the rest. His dreams pulled up at the roots. Being drawn by the will to survive. Treated like an animal, on the edge of madness. You move on with a clenched heart. No tears, your frustration has exploded inside of you. Your fears are dull because of their intensity. You have become immune to your fears. Pushed them inside of you, like a stuffed turkey. You are full of someone else's control. The Rubber Band man, How I wish I could comfort you, try to calm you're insanity. Your driving spirit is tenacious. So much love I have for you, so much empathy for you. Your broken heart is so obvious, your pain is deep inside of you consuming your whole world. Your ambition has been destroyed. But still, you continue to move. You have this quality, this strength. You are one of the lucky ones, not lost in your own self-pity. Rubber Band Man. You are so intelligent. Not willing to accept fate handed you. Never giving in to your depression and fears. Having so much courage to continue on in your struggle to be able to see a light at the end of the tunnel. In reality you are the only man. Having proven to yourself that you can't be kept down. That you can't be destroyed. You are one of the few endangered species. Rubber band Man so special so rare. This is describing what the black man has endured for over 400 years tragic.

Victim of Innocence

I was adopted into a family that was successful financially. My adopted mother was unable to show me love for whatever reasons she had. I never learned the value and appreciation of who I was. I suffered from low self-esteem from the very beginning. It was as if because I wasn't exactly like her, I was a failure. No appreciation or encouragement to be myself. I can't remember much but as this book moves forward this and memories will hopefully come back. I took dancing lessons. Singing lessons, piano lessons. Learned how to sew, to knit to be a good little girl. Then I started rebelling. Maybe because I was not getting approval and acceptance of who I was. Just a little hug once in a while would have made a difference. This account of my life is for all the young girls who grew up with a cold unfeeling mother. Sometimes I feel this is all she knew but she treated her real daughter differently so that idea went out the window. As far as being affectionate, oh hell no.!!! Not at all. My adopted dad was very kind and loving to me. Tried to show he loved me for myself. I cried so hard when he died. It broke my heart. I blanked out 99% of my childhood. Bits and pieces come back. I don't remember anything good. Isn't that a bitch. Getting raped and sodomized by the bastard that worked for my adopted Dad, started me on the road to self-destruction. I learned early that life was hard and couldn't trust anyone. I started drinking and became the town slut. Had gotten a very bad reputation. I couldn't tell one person about my rape. He threatened to kill me and my family. Since he worked for my Dad, I have seen him every day. I was 11 years old. He sat across the table from me. Glared at me and had me terrified. Of course I didn't tell my adopted mother because I knew she didn't give a shit. I suffered very badly physically and psychologically. No support. No one to talk to. The pressure got too much. My adopted mother got really cold. I started drinking and partying. Sneaking out. After I got raped life took a nasty turn. She sent me away to the city to work for some Jewish people and I started hairdressing school. I was just 15. Of course I messed that up. My mind was completely messed up. I was too young, plus got no counselling. I became a very angry young lady. I dropped out of school. I partied all the time. I met up with a pimp and off to Vancouver I went. I started selling myself and unfortunately got turned out. I was to heroin and started shooting it at 15 1/2. Before I knew it, I was addicted to heroin. I lived in Vancouver for a while. Got pimped by a piece of shit. He beat me, put me out in the street to pick up tricks, and took my money. Got me high on heroin. I worked in a whore house at 16. Had sex with hundreds of nasty men without protection. 5 dollars. Pathetic. Blow jobs and sex. It went on for a long time. Then finally I had enough. I ran off and started working the streets. I had to go through several experiences with terrible men that abused me in every way. Emotionally, mentally, and physically. Since I was addicted to heroin, it happened very quickly. I was injecting it, overdosing many times. I guess you can say I was lucky to have survived my addiction. Looking back. I must have had sex with over a thousand men before I turned 18. If there was anything to catch at that time I would have caught it. I worked in a whore house or two, having sex with 20 men a day. Our madam used to give us a penicillin shot once a month. No condoms. I had a pimp that took my money and gave me my daily injection of heroin. If I sound bitter, it's probably because I was for a long time. It wore off over the years, but I still feel the effect of it. It's like white on rice, it never goes away. I struggled for years to find a piece of myself. Just one piece. Couldn't relate had a terrible identity crisis. Being adopted, I didn't feel love from my adopted mother. That definitely contributed to my low self-esteem. I remember Vancouver, the underbelly, the streets, the whore houses, the dope houses. My memory is not great. I remember bits and pieces. I tried so hard to have a decent relationship with a man. My trust issues and low self-esteem wrecked that for me. I have serious trust issues; I've been alone since 1990. Even with friends and family, I'm always waiting for the knife in the back. It's very sad to have lived 72 years and not really feel close to anyone. I can't to this day hang onto anything, or anyone. I struggle to maintain friendships. I'm always let down I still have a few old friends. But sadly, I can't even trust them, that they are not talking behind my back. The emptiness in my life is deep, and I realize now what's become of what's left of me. Leftovers. I think back to when I was young selling myself and my soul.

Blood Bath Bar

I was hanging out with John. War vet. He had his .357 on his hip and I had my .22. We used to go to this bar called The Blood Bath. Several losers had been killed in there. I was living with Jesse at the time. I lived in housing with my two daughters, very young. We went to the bar that night, he parked up the street. Sat down in front of a big mirror at the bar. We were having fun and the next thing I knew this guy started yelling at John. It all happened so fast. He shot at him, just missing the back of my head. John turned around so quickly and shot him between the eyes. He slammed up against the wall, his damn eyes popped out. It was so shocking; John threw his keys at me and ran out. Shit, huh!! What the hell. The guy was dead laying on the floor. I ran out of the bar, took a few minutes to start the car. Went home back to the projects and laid low. After two weeks the police showed up at my door and arrested me. Took me to jail. I was there for a couple days, and John turned himself in. The real deal was self-defense. They let me go. I told them to keep my .22. This was a real eye opener for me to smarten up. My mother came and took the kids for the summer.

Took it like a man

Took my time in remembering when. It was so easy to pick up again. Life was a breeze easy and free. Now reality I can really see. For what it's worth, don't fool yourself into thinking you will always have your health. Trust me, in the blink of an eye you'll be almost ready to die. It's such a task to be so strong, after doing so much wrong. Wore myself out. Playing my games. Did so much wrong it was a damn shame. This world is such a risky place. Evil is this human race. Never before have we been so close. Pretty soon we'll all be toast. So, you see how silly it is to cry. Pretty soon we all will die. Atomic weapons, nuclear bombs. How the hell can we be calm? Try and forget your bull shit ways. Don't bother to count your numbered days. Life was fun back in those times. Now I'm paying for my crimes, of being young and so naive. What was I thinking to believe. That time would come when I would need. Another chance to succeed. I'm tired now, all used up for real. Knowing how bad it makes me feel. There is only one thing I can do now is count my losses and figure out how to move forward.

CHAPTER 2

FINDING MY WAY BACK

Finding my way back from hell took years. First of all, it took a long time to find myself. What was left of myself. This is a message for abused girls and women and the lack of self-love and low self-esteem. I look back now and when I stopped giving a shit whether people liked me or not that is when positive things happened. It's not that I don't give a shit but if I have to lose my image, my self-respect, my appreciation of myself or my love for who I am then it's just not worth it. There are millions of people in this world and if I can't find one person that loves me for who I have become then so be it. What's left of me then is perfectly ok with me. The moral of this story is mine first, ME FIRST!!!!!! When I can look at my soul and say what a beautiful person I am, imagine that. Without self-love nothing works. Everything comes after that. So be true to yourself. Even if you have to be alone. After all we are alone first. So, grow a set of balls and start reading this writing with an open mind. I hope the universe approves these words and help the people that can be helped by this book. Never give up your search for yourself.

This is the reality of what I am finding that is left of me. Emotional about the suffering in the world. I find I can cry for other people that suffer but hardly ever for myself. I am basically dead when it comes to my own emotions. I can feel for my animals. So, I guess this means I'm still alive lol. I have a wicked sense of humor. I laugh at weird shit lol. I have become an activist in some causes. Homelessness, drug addiction. Racism. Abused women and children. I have no patience or tolerance for liars. I hate phonies. Throughout my book I mention how harmful it is to lie. I have taken the things that I love the most in this world and made them the priority of why I get up in the morning. I push back the terrible feelings of nothing worth living for anymore. Not suicidal at all, just a heavy sinking feeling about what I have left of me. I find music therapy is my savior. I love music. Certain music only lol. Soul music. Most other music irritates the shit out me. I play the keyboard and write music. It takes me back to the days in my life when I had a normal appreciation of getting up and enjoying life. I struggle with isolation. Yes, I realize it is very difficult to let most people be too close to me. It is my biggest downfall. My inability to be able to trust. I mentioned throughout my book how valuable it is to have this positive element. Without the trust chip life is very fragile. I have spent most of my life by myself. No relationship. Not close to anyone. It is heartbreaking. I am 77 and realize my life is almost over. I can remember that when I was young, I ended up pushing people away. Somehow turning them off. It's like was my own worst enemy when it came to letting people in.

For occupying space

We all occupy space. Spiritually, mentally, physically and skillfully. This experience is completely different for each of us. Judging from the effects of the past, past lifetimes, we all have different experiences and memories. As an old woman, at 77, I have been through millions of experiences, good and bad, over the years. I have been given an awesome gift from the universe. I can read directly from the spirit world. Often they are shockingly accurate things I shouldn't even know. I have awareness of the deep meaning of occupying space. To start the process babies who are totally dependent on their caregivers are very fragile at this time in their lives. This is the time when our souls are still very connected to the spirit world. We are developed into forever identities depending on the love and acceptance we get. It forms our whole lives, our personalities, our whole being. To be raised without love leaves a very permanent fixed scar on the soul. It never leaves, as I have realized as I travel through this journey of life.

People occupying space. The damage done can never be repaired ever. White people have started to understand the harm done. No amount of time, No amount of I'm sorries, or money. If you are not white you have a problem. It's called subhuman treatment for over 400 years. I have seen it, felt it, and experienced it in its intensity. It is very scary, and the damage of having one's identity shredded is devastating. To be disrespected just for occupying space is why this book matters. This book also helps me to try to deal with my frustration and anger. Being mixed with Native Indian I have also experienced racism. Not even knowing why I was not given any respect. Especially in the summer when I would get darker looking more native. It was silent and personal. I would go into a store being watched just in case I would try to steal. Being talk at instead of talked to, respectively. Like I was tolerated instead of being appreciated for who I was. For occupying space, soulfully, spiritually, mentally. There is a deep personal hurt that can never heal when a person their whole life is not appreciated, or respected or loved just for occupying space. This has a very deep meaning. White people don't get it at all. I can say that there is a lot of white people that have recently started to understand the harm that has been done to people of color.

Closing Thoughts

I find myself very grateful for the life that I have created for myself. I found the reason to love myself years ago and that reason was simply I'm special. That's right Special. I love myself. Lol yes lol imagine that. I am at the stage in my life that I now understand what makes me tick. I know that I'm brutally honest. Too much for most people. I have survived horrendous experiences and changed the negative direction my life had gone. I'm ok now. This happened when I was a little girl. I'm now 77 years old. There are many young girls and women of all ages that have had horrible experiences they've been hiding for years. Pushing these emotions so deep that it is hard, almost impossible, to pull them out. I wrote these experiences down when I was in my 20's. I can't remember much anymore. There was a reason why these entries were saved for over 40 years. I had closed it many years ago. I hope to reach out to the women and girls that can't move forward positively. To give them hope. To show them loving yourself is the first ingredient in healing. Finding the little girl lost and trying to accept that there are pieces of yourself that will never be recovered. I hope this book is going to help start the healing process that is so necessary to begin a new positive and productive life.

Down to Earth Stuff

I'm falling asleep trying to write, but I have so much to say. This book will help many women that are willing to stop messing around. Wasting time on vanity, abusive relationships, and material things. I have been alone 24 years, all alone. No companion, no sex life. No f$&#k all. My choice. I ran or should I say ran every freaking potential friend or lover off that even tried to be around me. Why? Because they wanted something from me that I didn't have to give. Or I was just to raw for them. Nevertheless, I am who I am f%#&k it if the world don't like it. Apparently, it's my 275th time being here in this world. I realize this lesson I'm trying to learn is the lesson of trust. I realize that the only place I have been able to find trust and acceptance is with my pets. Pathetic huh? No, that is not where I want to go with my lack of trust. I rescue everything. I even hate to kill bugs. I hate taking a life and that is the way it is. I have two baby sparrows that I saved 2 years ago. Nippy and Lucky. Nippy the little, bigger bit me non stop while I was hand feeding him. Now they swing on their swings, looking in the mirror. Play with their toys and sing all day long. I have 15 birds. They are old and sick, some of them. Just like me. Half dead but trust me I have a strong spirit.

I love my pets. They love my music. They are with me until the end. If you are still reading this, give your hand a shake and pat on the back. It takes a strong, down to earth person to read and appreciate the truth.

In the long run

There comes a day in everyone's existence when you make the circle and recognize it. To find yourself at the beginning of the journey. Then you ask yourself what I have accomplished and what have I created. You know when you start looking for a reason for everything and everybody. That's when everything starts getting complicated. There is only one way in, one way out. Somewhere in the middle some of us turn back and some ride it out. There is somewhere in this continued education that we grasp onto the real meaning. Can understand the real meaning of why we keep changing and moving in other dimensions. When we finally discover that nothing ever stays the same. That is life becomes sweeter. I guess I've been through a thousand lifetimes, and it seems like this one was the least productive. But actually, it is an ever ending challenge for me to discover the next level of awareness. Curiosity to be intense. Time has helped establish a protective crust. This is only a protective device. I have found it so necessary to hide the softness within. I have tried exposing this vulnerable interior but have decided against it. My instinct tells me to cover up my real identity at times in order to survive against life's tricks. Yes, it has been a game for many people to be anything except the real them. By this I mean I mean defence mechanisms have become a part of everyone's life. They have been set up to prevent confusion and hurt. On occasions I find it possible to show and tell but very seldom can I do this without feeling a threat. This may be negative to some people but to me it is a must. The games people play are so numerous. Everyone has a different game to play for different reasons. Some of these games have a very ironic nature. Some of these games are backfiring on purpose. Isn't it strange that so many people are more afraid of themselves than anyone else. What has become of the beautiful 'I'm for real 'relationships. Showing kindness and warmth comes naturally for me. But it seems impossible to really get close to most people because of their inability to expose their real selves. Yeah, back to my trust chip is missing because of the horrendous experiences of my life. Now a days being trapped in this old body lol I find some comfort when I realize that time has dulled the pain and blocked many experiences good and bad. Memory that is a joke. Lack of it is a blessing. This book is not for me it is for the thousands of women that have been hurt and abused and are unable to move forward in a positive way. To start healing.

Inside Myself

There is a short fuse with a long memory. One way in, one way out. No turning back. Getting sick inside from frustration. Patience is worn thin. Understanding is on zero. I've washed my hands of the nightmare of my creation. It really tears me up to know. It really was a waste of time. As far as I'm concerned. This unconditional love is a poor excuse for reality. Everyone has a breaking point, a limit, and I've reached mine. I've a sickening feeling and I'm usually right. I can't let my heart be torn apart. I have to protect my sanity. Unbelievably shallow and cold. Now I have become bitter. In the knowledge that it's useless to continue to beat my head up against the wall. Because it's truly a lost cause.

My problem is trusting. It is so hard to go through life to have a freakin barrier around my soul. This writing is to help myself and other women to love themselves when you can't believe that anyone can. Does that make sense? Yes, loving yourself. Knowing who you are and what you have to give. I hate phony people and backstabbers. No way in hell can I trust a smiling face...that shows the evil lurking inside. I see more than most. I guess it's a gift, some people call it evil. I got it naturally. Super intuition. The biggest challenge. I have to have the staying power to even try to give people a chance. It is so terrible to have a fragmented soul, in pieces. The worst thing in life is not having any faith in another human being. I am totally tormented because I can't trust enough to let anyone close to me. To always feel the knife in my soul. I found that being alone for over 24 years. Eat alone, sleep, there is nobody at all. The emptiness of having my trust chip missing is unbearable and I been denial all these years. I find that every time I open my big freakin mouth the wrong shit comes out. Maybe I don't trust myself to say the right thing. I am not going to change for anyone. Be yourself, don't pretend to be someone else. The messed up thing is where I am in myself. To be able to search deep enough. To find myself buried in a whole pile of regret.

Neglect has such a Sour Odor

The sour odor of neglect suffocates the senses or was it the dry ice of disappointment that has burned and frozen my mind? Bitterness has captured my heart after having it twisted and broken. Oh, can't you see? Can't you see? The two sides of love. Ironic as it may seem it's weakness not strength that has the hypnotic control. Oh, can't you see the hypnotic eyes of love have destroyed my strength leaving me weak and vulnerable.

Our Truths

Where is your escape? Can you escape inside your dreams? You find yourself totally lost within your self made prison, a prison that has no compassion for you. The thing that you need the most is your worst nightmare. Can you visualize being free enough to let go? Locked in the bars that confine you there is nothing else. You find the elusive butterfly only to let it fly away. Out of reach the walls are hard so like a turtle you crawl into yourself, expecting to find the answer. It's frustrating to realize it's not there. You run deep, disappearing inside yourself. Searching, searching. Your expectations are more than you can stand. Scars of disappointment cloud your vision and almost destroy patience. Your greatest love has become an obsession. Driving you without mercy. Unable to be peaceful within yourself. Your like and spider caught in its own web.

Park View Hospital

My good friend turned me on to this Respiratory Therapy Class and showed me how to get a student loan. I lucked out and passed my GED exam after being out of school for years. I passed with a C average. Anyway, from there I started classes and what a trip that was. The theory part was hard as hell. They taught us everything right down to turning dead bodies inside out. I graduated with a B+ average. Don't ask me how I did it, maybe my determination to make something out myself. Since I had such a high average for that class l was one of the privileged ones that got to see a few autopsies. This is one of those experiences I'll never forget. I'll begin by telling you that the smell was a killer. Worse than cleaning chickens on a hot day. Unbearable!!! I don't know where I got the courage to stay, but I did. The man was sawing off the back of the head. He pulled back her scalp and then this big pile of brains, damn!!! Look like a bunch of grey noodles. By this time, I was really turned off. Then he started cutting up the intestines and throwing them in the sink. Too much!!! He acted like it was no big deal to him. Just chewing his gum and talking shit. I guess he had seen so many dead bodies that it didn't faze him any more. By the time he finished this woman was laying there with this big hole were guts used to be. Getting ready to be sent to the funeral home looking dead white. Full of cancer. This man cut out her spinal cord and lungs, full of white crater looking patches. Her lungs were dark bluish black. Enough to stop you from smoking. This was not the only autopsy I had to go through. They were all morbid as hell. Anyway, we lived through this and passed our exams. Then we were cut loose in the hospital. Lord have mercy poor patients, lol. We still didn't know shit and we were in for a hell of a surprise. Well, it was too late to turn back now. So, I had to go through with it. Now was the time to get serious, no more joking around. This was real shit. The really hard facts. Now I had no choice. I was sent to this hospital in the ghetto to begin my 6 month internship. I began my long and endless one on one situations with my patients. I can't remember their names anymore. Even their faces are hazy. One of the first days there I was put in the children's ward. Well, why did they do that I burst into tears right in front of everyone. Too soft. This 11 year old girl came in all broke up from a car accident. She was in really bad shape paralyzed. It tore me up to see her suffer. It was a very cold reality check. I watched how the interns and nurses were so hardened that it was heartbreaking.

My experiences as an intern were sometimes brutal. The lack of compassion at times was shocking. This nurse was making fun at this woman because they couldn't get the catheter to stay in place, saying her vagina was too big. I mean really. How cold can you get? This really amazed me, but it was just the beginning.

Anyway, the woman died and maybe she was better off. If she could have witnessed her code she would roll over in her grave. Another time I walked down the hall one evening and one of the old doctors was holding a stethoscope to the back of this old patient. He was telling her to breathe in and out. Telling her that her lungs were clear lol. Well, that was a real joke because he didn't even have the stethoscope in his ears. He was a real joke as a doctor. He only cared about the patients that he knew would live. He used to order a stat enema every morning for every one of his patients. He said that was the best treatment for people that don't breathe right. Who knows, maybe he was right about that, but his tactics were so freakin rude. Anyway, it is so obvious about the cruelty in certain situations in the hospital. I had four patients in ICU, sbout 15 patients to look after. One was an 80 year old man. Comatose. I was dealing with the MA1 respirator and an H cylinder hookup. I had to hook the double stage regulator to the vent, Shit. All by myself. I was damn nervous because I had just started working with life support and I wasn't that confident at this time. All of a sudden, the nurse's aide comes running down the hall. Code blue, Code blue. I thought to myself. Oh shit!! Now what? Anyway, I went into ICU. And I found my patient blue and not ventilating. When I bagged him, I realized the ET tube was jammed way down his throat. Well, this is the time that I realized that all the O2 in the world wouldn't help this patient. He was now starting to swell up, major fistula. Bullous emphysema. Shit I was scared. I called the supervisor, and he told me to extubate the damn patient and send him down to the morgue before anyone had a chance to investigate. Well, if this wasn't the coldest shit. Apparently, the nurse's aides were in ICU and turned the patient while changing the linen. When they turned him, they unhooked him from the vent and accidentally pushed the ET way down his throat causing a fistula. What a bummer. Well, they never had an autopsy on the old man. What it boiled down to was the stupidity and carelessness of the aide. The boss said he was just vegetative anyway. That resulted in the premature death of that old man. This was how my internship went. It was a quiet hospital. We had many gunshots patients. This young kid 17 or so, Ghetto kid, came in. His 14 year old brother had just died from getting shot in a gang fight in South central Los Angeles. He was shot in the chest 5 times. We had to do an open cardiac massage on him. He coded 3 times. We had to rush him off for open heart surgery. He barely survived. He stayed in the hospital. 3 months. Finally, he went home. 10 days later he was shot in the head. We tried to save him, but he was too far gone. Sad. The gang bangers were wild back in 1982. The brothers all died in that family.

This internship I did was completed at 3 different hospitals in South Central LA. I was really shocked at the gruesome reality of autopsies. Anyway, I don't know how the pathologists do it. I mean everyday pulling out people's guts. Shit!!It was all too freakin morbid for me. Well let me tell you there were 7 of us dummies that went down to the morgue with our gowns and masks. I was scared when I looked over on this hard cold steel table and seen this dead woman lying there. Shit I almost split right then. I thought to myself, you know this is not for you. But anyway, I talked myself out of it and stayed to watch the gory mess. I will tell you as I remember after all it's been 8 years since this happened and my memory isn't the best. This pathologist took a knife and stuck it right in the woman's chest. Shit!!! All this horrible smelling stuff came running out all over the woman's chest. Then he cracked open her ribs and pulled them back like she was a chicken. Then he politely started cutting out all the body parts. First the liver and the gall bladder and put it on the sink. By this time, I ran out and got damn sick.

Missing Piece

Knowing what I know now. I would have done things a bit differently. I think seriously about the path that I went on and the quicksand of regret, of the frustration of not being able to find that missing piece of my soul. It's deadly. There is something that happens to victims of abuse at a young age like I was. It's like a piece missing. Not that I can't find it, it's like it's broken into a million pieces. That piece contained all the torment and pain, but it can't be fixed. All the pieces are shattered and unfixable. My memories come in bits and pieces. They are frozen in time. I can't put them in order. I can't put them in a time frame. I'm alone and not feeling close to anyone. My daughters are cold to me but I really cannot waste any energy on that. I've been losing memory lately, short term is gone. There was a shadow in the doorway, hanging around waiting. The morning light has cornered it sent the shocks of reality through it. Rushing to fast to be productive there also is stillness, a quietness, a haunting echo hovering over it. Remembering when tomorrow is so we're ripe, ripe with the knowledge of creativity. Weighing the heaviness of the situation. Being bogged down with other folks hangups is a useless waste of energy and emotion. Never being fruitful enough too glow in the dark but must emerge into the light. All this inner turmoil.

Rawness of My Life

I struggled for years to find my identity. Being adopted did not help. I could never piece myself together to discover my identity. Without all the pieces there is not much hope of that. So besides having low self-esteem I had an identity crisis. I remember Vancouver, the under belly. The streets, whore houses, and dope houses. The trouble is my memory comes in spurts. I can't remember much. I tried so hard to have a relationship with a man. I couldn't then and even now, been alone for over 20 years. I have serious trust issues. Even with friends. I always wait for a knife in my back. It's really sad to have lived 67 years and not feel close to anyone. I can't to this day hang onto nothing., or a friendship. I struggle to maintain friends, but they always let me down. I still have a few old ones, but rarely do I feel that I can actually trust them. That they are not talking behind my back. That's messed up, huh. The emptiness of my life is deep, and I realize what's become of what's left of me. Leftovers. I think about when I started selling my butt and soul. I must have had sex with over 1000 men before I turned 18. Isn't that a bitch. I also was a real slut if I wasn't in some shitty relationship. My relationships never lasted long very sad.

Reality of Truth

Oh yeah. Excuse my French. But I don't give a rat's butt whether you like it or not. This book is about the reality of abuse. Self-abuse and by bastards that just didn't care. My childhood was so empty of love. I can't remember that emotion or where to find it even now. Is there anyone that can live alone without love? And if you have and survived what is left of this shell. Empty shell. Understanding love, everyone thinks they know what it is. In order to love. Trust has to be there within yourself before even thinking about trusting someone else. The ability to be vulnerable. To let someone else have the freedom that will affect you. If there is no trust, then life will never happen. I have to try to figure out why anyone could possibly like me, then if they act like it's possibly true but then I have to try not to test them to actually come close to actually believing it. It's very sad to have the trust chip missing, malfunctioning. My trust goes as far as eye contact lasts, then it's gone. The sad thing about this world is that people are too freaking shallow a lot of the time. There is only so deep they will go then they will punk out. You know I'm suffering even now at 67. I don't have friends because I don't trust anyone. How sad.

REALLY?

Shallow or denial. Huh???? Which one??This book is not for the weak minded. Grow a set of balls or please put the book down. Life in the fifties and sixties was not supportive for abused girls and woman. It was like, oh what did you do? To deserve that. I have evolved into a very emotional strong old woman. 72 years of life living it my way. I have learned over the years you can't depend on other people for your happiness. They might be able to enhance it, but happiness comes from us. Our own ability to find something within ourselves to be able to appreciate our own uniqueness. As we look in our mirror we have to look from our third eye. This special awareness is necessary to be able to find our true selves. The ability to find the strength to move above the toxic nightmare we find ourselves trapped in sometimes. Whatever reason that has trapped us in a self- made prison. A prison that has locked our own uniqueness in its quicksand of negatively. A toxic mold on our souls from pushing stuff inside and not dealing with reality. Personally, I have forgotten far more than I can remember which might be a good thing in terms of self-preservation. A sinking feeling about my past haunts me and no ghost hunter will be able to hide the spirit of this hideous reality. Yes, this book is deep. I dig deep. Too deep to touch anymore. It's just like watching a 3D movie. I know now I'm damn lucky to still be breathing and having evolved into a very strong woman. A bionic woman lol. I have no tolerance for liars and phonies. I am alone with my pets. Animals can teach us a lot about being for real. Emotional honesty is something that a lot of people know nothing about. It's damn scary.

Searching (inside your love)

There is more to it than a passing fantasy. I need much more than a lick and a promise. I run too deep for just touching, it's got to be something from your soul, down to the bone. I see without my eyes and feel without my hands. I don't need them. They are only physical. They get in the way of me getting the real thing. I searched my heart for the reasons why I'm still alone; and what it is I'm desperately trying to find. I have always known that I'm different, and when I try to play the game to fit in, I get lost. I need a spiritual healing, and I have to have a man that has the sensitivity that it takes to set me free. There is nothing in this world that I really need except my own awareness of my personal growth. I learned that I could jump tracks and still absorb the benefits of all the solitude and meditation. I can stand this empty void and understand why it's there; but I can't erase this pain or turn back the wasted years. I only have my own strength to stand on and sometimes I feel so tired. I really need a place I can go and escape from the world. Somewhere safe and warm. Somewhere that I don't have to worry about being left by myself. Somehow, I find that thought weak because I've always felt alone. Why should it bother me so much now? I guess time has a way of changing people. Sometimes for the worse. Sometimes time creates a bond that sterilizes all insecurities without anything but my own mental and emotional abilities.

Secrets of my soul

The goal of my book is to help in the healing of the many abused young girls and women who are lost. I know that the words in this story of my life will touch the souls of many. I know because the meaning is so deep that it can't be softened. I have suffered so much as a young girl, young woman that no amount of time can ever erase the rawness of it. I get flashbacks from time to time. It's like wow did I really survive this nightmare. Physically yes, but my soul has been damaged. I can remember being afraid and alone. I could not help myself because of my addiction to heroin. I was 16 with a 100 dollar a day habit in 1960. Lots of money. I was willing to do anything for it. All I cared about was getting high. I sold my butt on the street. Stood on the corner all night. Rain or shine. It was a very dangerous time in my life. I jumped in cars with anyone. Strangled; pushed out of moving cars. I had the shit beat out of me. It was a miracle that I even survived. I had no love for myself. No self-respect. I was a drug addict and a thief. I used to go to these expensive stores and steal anything I could get my hands on. I never got caught. Stole expensive clothes, sold them and dressed myself up like a movie star. Lol. Yeah right. So addicted to heroin it was pathetic. Sleeping behind garbage cans, so high I would pass out and be at everyone's mercy. I overdosed many times almost died. Shooting heroin, speed cocaine. Yeah. I worked in a whore house for a while. Turning tricks for 5 dollars, half and half 7. Imagine having sex with 20 or more men a day. 20 times 5 is 100 dollars for having 20 men abuse me. Then my pimp would take all my money and take me to the dope house, and I would get high all night on 5-10 dollars. Pathetic. I only had a pimp for a little while. 3 months or so. I was too addicted to heroin. So, the reality of these horrific years remains forever in my soul. I never was able to come back fully from those years on the street. Sometimes even now at 75 years old I can actually feel the pain of those times. I talk to girls sometime and ask them why you don't try to get clean, the answer is I just want to get high. I have realized that without self-love I might as well be dead. Loving myself, I discovered was the thing that saved me. I was able to pull myself out of years of abuse, abuse by others and self-abuse. Self- abuse is a very sad reality. Not being able to find nothing within myself to love, appreciate, or respect. Very sad. Getting raped at such a young age, not being able to get any help, not one person I could tell. That left a dent in my soul. Being raised without love or affection was very emotionally hurtful. I know any girl or woman on the street is definitely suffering from lack of self-love. I hope my pain and suffering will be able to help others through my writings.

Soul's Journey

This book is about regret too. The sadness of knowing that all the efforts I made to be close to someone failed. Every last one of them. I have a short endurance for the ability to even try to reach out and feel. No that has all been somewhere else, some other lifetime. Someone else can relate to that. Every day, love exists everywhere. Where's mine? My turn to feel. This book is not about positive and negative. It's about the reality of a damaged soul, and how it can survive in this freakin shallow society. The society game, oh yeah. I used to play it. Now I'm very impressed to find the energy to even pretend to care. I'm a natural all the way. I realized years ago why the hell should someone care about what they look like. I say that because I know I don't. I wash my butt, brush my teeth and that's it, lol. Program myself to keep moving forward in a somewhat positive way. I love my pets and would do anything for them. They are my lifeline to love. They are loyal and so emotionally honest. I would spend my lifetime, what's ever left, with my pets, my babies. I really want this book to be about my life and experiences. To clear the fog outta my soul and try to help other damaged souls. I'm so weak in some ways, stronger than most in many others.

The Roller Coaster Ride. Did you think it was going to be smooth? Oh, get a grip on it. That's not the way life it. Up and down, down and up. Around the corners, over the humps. That's the easy part. What about the fight to stay on board? Oh yeah that's the big one. There was no guarantee. Where did you think you were going? Money couldn't save you; all it did was camouflage reality. There is a certain wisdom in knowing. The ride would always end up the same way no matter how you got there. You meet the same people going up as you meet coming down. Allowing yourself to escape is a big mistake. Feel the rawness of it instead. You can never protect yourself with material things. Financial gain is such a disappointment. I've tried to warn you, but you wouldn't listen. Protect your mind from the cold. You're better off, it's more beneficial. Forget about things for a moment. Can you get to heaven in a Cadillac? Why waste so much time? Searching for Fool's Gold.

The Straight and Narrow.

Such a hard path to follow. So difficult to find. But you will know immediately. It's all so simple. So uncomplicated. Detachment is the solution. To become more aware of the tragedy of loss. It's better not to have. We are only borrowing and using it, even for our children. Nothing is ours to keep. No man, woman, or child can save you from yourself., from you're future. So, to not waste any more time building up bad karma. Yeah, the boomerang of life, so accurate so revengeful. Coming back to you with such a vengeance. So easy to get off track, to get lost. Losing our way. The elusive butterfly. It's like a needle in a haystack.

Memories come to me crying. Lost in Space and Time, caught up in it like quicksand suffocating all the senses and walking dead over your soul. The masquerade is over.

Running in circles chasing your tail you fell into your own trap , expecting to find the vision. What you were escaping from has caught up with you. Let go of this bitterness. Give yourself a chance. You bite the hand that feeds you. Standing alone in your hangups escaping into your delusions of grandeur confused between fantasy and reality. All this destruction has no limits. No boundaries. Only uncontrolled thoughts. Only in the dream state do you feel alive. Only then do you have some purpose. Memories have been faded and weak.

Stone Cold Reality

As the years went by, I slowly started liking myself. It's like I lost my hopes, dreams and direction along with my self-respect. I had to learn to trust myself and everyone else. It was the worst feeling to lose faith in humanity. The reality was the more I disliked and abused myself was the more I had sunk into a vicious cycle of self-destruction. Couldn't find one thing to give me a reason to even try to fix myself. I attracted the worst life had to offer. Very abusive men. Controlling, judgmental. Two faced, backstabbing, very violent. They had little respect for themselves and women. I had to get pregnant with my daughter to end it. I tried for years to get my trust in people in general. It was very difficult. Even to this day I can't trust very much. Always waiting for the knife in my back. Now in my early 70's I have decided to write these memories and try to help other girls and women. My whole life I have never been able to hold onto anything. Never been able to finish anything. Or continue on my journey. It's because of my low self-esteem. The depth of my inability to trust or have faith in my own ability to succeed. No respect for myself, anything or anybody.

The Mistake

Regretting my bad decision

Never can I love another man and give as much of myself as with you. You see, I have grown very impatient with people, especially men. There is no way that I can replace what has been destroyed by bitter experiences. I've tried but it's useless. You see, you were my everything. And now I have no desire to give to another man. Maybe one day, maybe somehow l will be able to erase the bitterness and distrust I have within me. Maybe there will be a man that will understand why I'm like I am. I can't seem to shake this depression I feel when I think about my marriage to you. There wasn't any way to explain to you how badly I was hurt.; and besides that, every time I look at you baby, I realize you were hurt too. If only we could have tried harder to understand each other and tried to make it work. Maybe someday you will be able to forgive me for leaving you and try to understand why I did it. Why did I have to get away from you? I will never be able to love another man again until you help me with this guilt I feel. You know years have gone by and I still feel the same way about you. You were my man. Only you could understand me and make me feel secure. Now it's over and I have finally realized that I can't turn back the hands of time. Maybe later on I'll be able to try to love again. There are moments when I desperately need you, even now. If only I could have known, then what would become if my life? You will never know just how sorry I am. Because you won't give me a chance.

Yesterday was beautiful. Yesterday was my whole existence. Yesterday's mistakes cost me something that can never be repaired. Your love lingers on through all the pain and emptiness. Having been foolish in losing you is something I'll never get over. My whole existence is shattered. The world doesn't even exist. You were all that ever mattered. You were everything to me. My lover, father, brother, sister, and mother. You see love life doesn't mean anything to me now. I have made a foolish mistake that cost me my happiness. You are gone but those beautiful memories still remain to torture me and remind me of my mistake. You were my man, my only man. You were my whole world. I know now that I hurt you very deeply when I left you alone. You had too much pride for one man. You were too proud to tell me to come home. Oh baby, it's too late for us. Too late for love, and too late for me. You were what I needed. You see baby I was too stupid to realize that. Now it's too late.

The Process of Healing

Over the years I realize that I have been permanently changed. My life had taken on the journey of finding the little girl lost. There were many times over the years when this mentality of very low self-esteem had been the controlling force in my life. My decisions were based on bad judgement, a behavior that changed over the years. As a young girl I never thought about the consequences of my actions. Severely damaged emotionally, I survived terrible abuse. Emotionally. Mentally, Spiritually. I really had no respect for anything including myself. It took getting pregnant to shock me back into the reality of my own self abusive behavior. I found that over the years I haven't been able to complete anything or hang on to anything. I couldn't finish what I started. I tried but seemed to turn off myself and everyone around me. I discovered that without self-love I couldn't complete my goals. I tried for years but failed on most attempts. Learning how to love myself was the first ingredient in healing. I found that trying to find anything about myself that I could respect and appreciate was almost impossible. It was a slow process but one morning I woke up and I had changed. No longer fighting myself. Accepting the leftovers as the new me. This is when my life started taking a turn for the better. Getting back my self-trust, respect. Appreciation of who I had developed into.

Reality Check

It's like I had this wild hair up my ass, lol. It's like I had this driving force inside of me to never be able to chill, to settle down. I tried several times. Always searching for something. You know to this day I still don't know what the hell it was, but I know what I found to replace it. Myself. I found my own worst enemy. I looked high and low for me but honey I was lost in space. Not out there tweaking but just kind of trying to escape the reality of my life. I had my fun if I don't get well no more. You know that saying has some very deep undertones. Sometimes when we are young, I think we just kind of float through life expecting to have this great big dream about the future come true. I never thought that one day I'd be sitting here with just as many regrets as humanly possible.

I guess some people are much more into material things, and really sit down and worry about the emptiness of life. They couldn't give a shit if the moon turned to blue cheese. They need to go to the lost and found and turn themselves in because life to me is much more than material comfort. Financial gain to me is just one of the mistaken wastes of time in this society. You've got to work, work your ass off for 30 years, 50 years. Then finally your house is paid for. Then a couple years later you die.

Duh. To me something don't seem quite right about that concept. So, working 3 months to pay off an $800 table. Why not go to Goodwill and pick up one used for $80 dollars? Use the rest of the money to see the world or save it for hard times. Everyone needs money to survive. But a lot of people put money as their main priority, and then they lose track of the real reason for being here. What has nothing to do with material things. I sometimes believe people that are so materialistic really don't believe in the afterlife. How could they? A lot of rich people, don't really care about the person next door, never mind the rest of the world. I guess a lot of people might say I'm negative and cynical about life, but to me my evaluation is quite accurate. I'm bitter about certain things but I would rather use the words fed up. I don't have time for other people's hangups. I believe even if you help someone carry their burden some of the way. They are going to have the same problem alone. So, to me it's just putting off the inevitable.!

The Reality of Life

I'm sitting here at 1 am messed up because someone is driving me nuts with their shitty taste in music. I still play my music loud when I'm in the mood. Music calms the beast in me. Well now if you are still reading this craziness then you really need to accept the fact that you are a real human being...To be able to understand what I'm trying to say here. It's about finding and picking up the pieces of what's left after self-destruction. Actually, I like myself. To look in the mirror and see the real deal. I look like a dried up old woman in my pics...lol. but that is not who I see in the mirror. Except on the days when I really feel sick. The mirror of our soul. Our eyes tell everything. Eyes are really the entrance to the spirit world. Our third eye. I can see things. Get messages and information from the spirit world. And no, I am not delusional or schizoid. I'm just a person that has been gifted from the spirit world with an extra sense. I used to run from it because it was damn scary. I can read minds, not always, but when the path is clear. It is very easy for me to see through someone. I surprised myself just saying things that turned out to be true. It is a gift, not something evil or crazy. We only use a small fraction of our brain. This extra sense has saved my butt on many occasions. If I'm in danger I can sense it immediately. If someone is playing games, I know immediately. Even before they know. It's really intense but it's true.

The Straight and Narrow

It's such a hard path to follow and so difficult to find, but you will know immediately when you have.

It's all so simple, so uncomplicated. Detachment is the solution to become more aware of the tragedy of loss. It's better not to have as we are all borrowing and using it, even down to our own children. Nothing is ours to keep. No man, woman or child can save you from yourself, from your destiny. So, don't waste any more time building up bad karma. Yeah, the boomerang of life. So accurate, so revengeful, coming back at you with such a vengeance. So easy to get off track? To get lost losing our way. The elusive butterfly. It's like a needle in a haystack.

Yesterday No Matter What

Building onto my knowledge and sometimes getting stuck climbing the stairway. The road is so hard to find and hard to stay on. Memories can work either way. Using them for a smoother ride and a level of comfort. Don't get lodged in a time warp. These are the last days just passing through in reality. Are you going to waste any more time? Come on baby, time is up. Let's get down to the nitty gritty. Father time done played a game on mother nature. Oh yeah, the vision is so haunting. Blinding me is driving me forward. Don't play with me, because I need you and need you badly. Cause there is only what is real. In my next breath along with my dreams. God knows how hard it's been. Never ease up on your thoughts of me. Because I need your strength, so we can move on through. And catch the reality of the here and now. And leave it behind in our memories.

The Struggle is Real

This struggle of fighting myself, fighting my insecurities, my lack of self-love, my confidence to succeed in life and my trust issues. I so desperately needed someone to say "Darlene, you can do this. You can finish this. Don't stop, this is good". But the words never came. The words I so desperately needed to continue in my struggle to find something, anything to give me the confidence in myself, in ability to complete my goals. To have faith in myself to finish what I start. I'm aware now that I was broken. It took me years to learn to trust myself. To trust anyone. To this day at 72 it is still very hard for me to trust. I have gotten to the point in my life that I have accepted, finally accepted that I will never recover this piece of myself. This broken piece. Trust is very fragile. It is so important to me to be able to find that piece, that tiny piece, to help in my struggle. To be able to trust anything or anybody. It is still difficult for me to look in the mirror. The mirror of my soul and say "Darlene you can do this". I live one second at a time. The future is not there past my next breath. I find this acceptance of the reality of my life is the only way for me to feel safe. This is how I maintain control. One second at a time. The ironic thing is that I like myself, lol. This is now this second in reality. I like who I have developed into. I force myself everyday to be strong.

My strength comes from my awareness of the fragile nature of trust issues. I'm aware now, especially now at 72 with my trust chip missing it changes everything. Without trust I could never be close to anyone. I always waited for the knife in the back. I'm always surprised when someone can push past my barrier. Even for a second. I'm always surprised when I think that someone can like me for myself. I'm very blunt, brutally honest. I realize now that my gift of incredible intuition and supernatural abilities is a gift from the universe. The universe gifted me with a higher degree of awareness and sensitivity. I will always be grateful to the universe for allowing me to access the mysteries of life.

The deep and mind blowing realities of this life that I'm so aware of. This new me. This awareness of this gift of knowing that has saved me from myself, the harm and danger that I had put myself in over the years. This awesome gift that I will discuss later in more detail. This is not just for me, it's for everyone that exists. Life has a very brutal way of showing us that we are messing up. I always get my karma right back. Slaps me right in the face. Even now at 72 I am so aware of what I do. It is like a strong awareness of what I'm creating for myself. I have become aware of my ability to keep looking forward to another minute, another day. I've spent 90% of my life alone. I can't accept anyone that can't be honest about their feelings. I absolutely hate liars and phony people. I can see right through it. I'm so brutal with my honesty that people avoid me sometimes especially when I am ready to crash and burn. I love to be able to let it all hang out. I refuse to waste another minute on people that are delusional about who I am. What I have to offer, my abilities, my gifts the universe has so kindly given me. This book will help whoever can get past their fears and grow a set of balls. I'm very strong mentally, spiritually, and emotionally. My health is not so good. I suffer pain every day. Pain is a bitch. Pain management. Enough of my health issues, I'll get back to that later.

The Truth

When I know something is too much, I end it. Whatever it is, whatever it takes, I end up in a place that I have to appreciate or else lose my damn mind. That is 100% correct. Lose my freakin mind. I have to accept my fate. The end result of my inability to look into the future. Long term, short term. Freak that. There is no time on sh!t. Day to day, hr. to hr., minute to minute. I would like to find a better place to live. I am surrounded by a bunch of drug addicts. Tormented souls. drunks. violent and angry. Freaking cockroaches and mice. aren't that a bitch. It's all my own doings, nobody else's fault, just my own dumb assed decisions. I am so down to earth don't abuse drugs or alcohol. I don't go anywhere, to party or hang out. A loner. I am in a situation now in my life that I can't pretend to even think I'm ok. Well, what I mean by that is that I'm in a shitty place in my life right now. No money, bad health, no friends, no partner. Just me and 4 cats, 2 little dogs and 15 birds. I love music, soul music only. Blues oh yeah. I can relate to that. It pulls be back from my anger and frustration. You know I know the formula to make it right for myself. But I can't find the damn ingredients. You know life can be simple, uncomplicated. The only thing is I don't have the money to be comfortable. well now, that is just too bad, aren't it? I'm not starving, my pets are spoiled, fat and never miss meals. It is a financial problem. But I am ok.

There is No Coming Back from Rape

All the counseling in the world cannot bring back innocence. All that counseling does is try to show a way to accept and move forward. Rape should carry a death sentence. The victim has a death sentence of trying to find the leftovers. Leftovers of what used to be. This is not an exaggeration of reality. The reality of rape is something that stays with the victim forever. It took me over 20 years to start dealing with my anger instead of stuffing it down. 20 long years. I hope that the girls and women that read my writing will be able to feel the depth of it. Deep inside. Find a place where you will be able to start healing. It will never come back 100% but with time finding that new person inside. That new woman that has now found a love for herself. It takes a long time to get to the place where looking in the mirror and loving that woman looking back at you. It changes everything. Finding love and appreciation for myself was so deep. I just woke up one morning and realized that everything was going to be alright. I could trust and depend on myself again. I loved the woman that I had developed into. Most people cannot understand me or who I am inside. I am brutally honest. I am kind. Love animals. But don't piss me off lol. I am a bitch from hell if I'm pushed too far. Lol I hate liars. Mean people. I just want to live my life, what's left of it peacefully. Having gone through so much in life I can't let most people in but still I try to be helpful and kind. So, you see how and what it takes to begin the process of coming back. Finding oneself. Never give up. It is so beautiful and brings on an extra deep level that is even sweeter. Trust to me is the most important thing in a relationship along with honesty and sincerity. I cannot let most people in. I have tried but it just doesn't work for me. I have spent over 90% of my life alone, even though people were in my life. I still was alone. Sad.

What's Real

You float through life like an illusion. Can you control that silly smirk? Or are you too disgustingly selfish? But where are you without self-love? Or are you to shallow to comprehend? Is it the entire structure of humanity that needs a little more soul? If you, had it? I mean the elusive butterfly of life, could you catch it, or let it get away? Sweeten up your sour grapes. camouflage your insecurities. Is life a parade of smiling faces? Maybe the actors forgot their lines, disguising their confusion, hoping for a better tomorrow. What will emerge from the darkness? A hideous monster? Feelings too deep to reach? Bring your disappointment to the surface and tell the world to go to hell if they don't like it. Can you make yourself smile? Or are your hangups eating you up.? Look in the mirror and visualize a happy face. They say I'm silly. They say I'm crazy. But I don't need them to make me smile.

Lost in Space

How ironic the spider is caught in his own web. The only thing that you love has become too much for you. Where is your escape as yourself destruct? You search for freedom in your dreams, but they only drive you to destruction. Totally lost in your self-made prison, you disintegrate and disappear within yourself. Trying to hold it together you lose ground slipping into the quicksand of your bitterness. Just like a snake your blood runs cold and there aren't any feelings in your heartless soul. You're like a vampire empty of all compassion, searching for your next victim. You've become like dry ice burning a hole in your soul. Your karma has become almost dangerous. It's a heavy load you're carrying and never once have you stopped to think you're programed like a computer. Like an animal you are cunning, self-preservation is your goal. Your lack of sensitivity is frightening. You suffer from delusions of grandeur. Masquerading as a peaceful soul. You're a master at camouflage, camouflaging true emotion. Or should the truth be known, lack of it. Afraid of losing control you won't let go. So now like a walking dead man you move living on the edge of madness. You maneuver yourself through life, playing it like a chess game. Exploiting and dismissing. Lost in space and time. Caught in it like quicksand. Suffocating all senses, walking dead over your soul. Running in circles chasing your tail. You fell into your own trap expecting to find the vision. What you were escaping from has caught up with you. You have no shame in your game. You played yourself, no more fooling mother nature. Realizing father time has gotten rude.

CHAPTER 3

LEFTOVERS

How do people go through their lives and live in a phony bubble? To me it's such a waste of energy being phony. I am well aware of the reality that what is left of me is very damaged. But I have saved myself because I have to share this reality with all the woman that have self-love problems. I healed myself but it took a lot of being brutally honest about my life.

Many years ago, my life was a nightmare from hell. Surviving for almost 10 years on the streets of Vancouver. Sleeping behind garbage bins. Overdosing, almost dying many times. I'm a different kind of old lady. These stories are about survival. I believe there was a reason for me to be here today and I hope reading my writing will save many girls from selves, from continuing to move in such a negative direction. The most important thing in this world is self-love. The ability to be able to find something in myself to love and value. I'm almost 76 now. Old fart lol. I live alone with 3 cats, a fat little dog and 2 birds. They are my world. I am pretty well isolated. After this pandemic I have changed. I think everyone has. I find my patience is on zero. I can't tolerate phony people, liars, shallow people. I personally prefer animals to people. It's true they show their true feelings, expose their souls. We can learn a lot from them.

My strength comes from my pain and suffering. My solitude. I made this prison, the one I put myself in years ago. I became another person after my rape. I hope the women that read this will get the real meaning of my words. Don't waste time messing around pretending. Pretending to be someone you're not. Pretending to feel something you don't. Trying to impress people with BS. The delusional thoughts. Delusions of Grandeur. What the hell. Was it that important to lose who you are? Nobody. You have to be who you are. Who you have become. The new you. The leftovers of being freaked around by everyone. Poor little me. My butt!! I'm too strong to give in to self-pity. This is about helping other women that have not been able to succeed in finding out the truth about themselves. Their full potential was never reached or even got close to because if the lack of self-worth and the inability to trust. It is so messed up, isn't it? Who can I turn to, who can I remember? I have to search my archives to pull out one or two over the years that penetrated my barrier. This feeling I have now at 67 is very honest. I have found out who I really am, not what other people have fantasized about. I'm me, the one that had always been there, but unfortunately was buried many years ago. I'm strong enough to refuse to give up and try to look at the positive side of things.

Leftovers from Rape

It's all about the leftovers. That time has come and gone. No one could hear or care about the cries from within the boundaries of reality. I have learned by the pieces scattered, judging from the trail of destruction. I should have known this would happen but you can't miss what you never had. What never existed in time to do any good? What a nightmare to realize the years gone by were empty of compassion. To actually to have existed in a bubble, the very life was sucked out of any hope to be part of something to belong. Instead, it was pathetic failed attempts. How did I even think this life would be different? I realize I have a fractured soul, fractured by failed attempts to feel worthy of love. The reality of my lack of trust. Understanding now that was my biggest downfall. I trust no one, not even myself. I pull my strength from myself. My stubbornness to survive. Day by day, hr. by hr. minute by minute. The real understanding of the reason my existence has been so brutal. When trying to let people in. Failed attempts to bond, to allow another soul to penetrate my boundaries. Without trust that can never be. Unfortunately, the time has come and gone, the time that really mattered has expired. The new change from within, now without allowing any penetration of my barrier.

Let It Go

When the negative and positive are trying to occupy the same space, it's impossible. There is no way to expand. Sweeping out the endless dust of the past, knowing it will all be back tomorrow. We must rise out of destruction. The same old patterns must be broken. We can't allow that haunting thing to be controlled and have no room for other people's hangups in our existence. Because of the dangers of choices, we must isolate and pressure. We can never tolerate a wasted chance. Hold onto your dreams and get out of the way. Try to wiggle free from yourself made prison? Let yourself catch a glimpse of infinity. Nothing stays the same. Everything must change. Do you remember what was left, preserved and kept? Locked in place for eternity. It's your identity, a special individual spirit. I know we run deep and have weight intolerance because of the heavy reality we have survived. Can't you see the escape is right in front of you? Like a spider caught in its own web you can't seem to free yourself from the quicksand of your bitterness.

Looking Back

Judging from my attitude and frame of mind I can only say that this is what is left of me. I can't tolerate any bullshit. I have zero patience and acceptance of phonies. I smell a rat in one second. I find that I am the product of a horrendous childhood. Street life. Prostitution. Abuse physically, mentally and emotionally. What's left of me now is an old lady without a filter. It's a daily struggle for me to socialize. Most days I prefer to be alone. My pets are my life. I live for them. I prefer animals, they are emotionally honest. I can trust them. Trust is the most ingredient in a relationship.

Yesterday

Yesterday I met you and your beauty. Yesterday has become today with its strength. Yesterday has become part of tomorrow. Your love was like a cloud floating through me taking me higher. Your love has become a necessity. Loving someone that is not mine. Loving on borrowed time. My need for you exceeds my desire to stay away. As I wait, knowing it is all in vain. Looking out into emptiness, seeing only loneliness and memories of what used to be. There are times when the sweetness takes over and all the ugly things are erased for a while. It becomes easier to let go and enjoy the peacefulness that comes when love is expressed to the fullest. To be able to love without destroying. To be able to accept love without possessing it. One can only get love when it is given freely and can only give love when it is natural. Love cannot be demanded or possessed. The only way to keep love is to let it be free to grow

Where is the elusive Butterfly

Are you blind? Or can you find it? The elusive butterfly of your mind. Can you hear or do you fear? The sounds of the universe. Isn't it time to search for the rhyme and reason for your existence? How long will it be before you see it? Your inevitable ending. You're life's not worth a dime. Why waste your time, searching for Fool's Gold

Having made it this far and shockingly still have a functioning sense of reality is amazing. Because of my brutal honesty people have run far away from me. I'm running on fumes for as a while now. I can't understand how anyone can waste any time looking for Fool's Gold. I can only tolerate the raw truth about anything. I am in severe chronic pain. Everywhere in every nook and cranny. I am on pain medicine. It is not helping that much anymore. Walking is getting very hard. I now fight depression from the horrible pain that I endure 24 hrs. a day. At my age having gone through hell and endured the evil experiences that have made me what I am today.

The Last Chapter

This book is for the young women and girls that will never be the same again. Fractured souls, looking to find the broken pieces. Even then the vessel will never look or be the same. This is the last chapter. This is the closure for my broken life. This is the last chapter about a broken soul. I have discovered the only salvation for me was to find something about me that I could be proud of. Not depending on anyone else for approval. I took a deep look with my third eye into what was actually left of me. What is left is an old lady who can appreciate myself, love myself. Imagine that. The world is a nasty place sometimes. The shelter that we all need came from me. Within myself I found a switch that I learned to turn off and on. It turned off to anything or anyone that pushed my buttons my survival buttons. My " love myself" button. I turn it on only when I feel safe. I find my fur babies talk to me, "turn it on for us Mom". People can learn a lot from animals about being for real. Emotional honesty.

This is definitely the truth and the details of my life. I hope it will help abused women and girls. The worst thing ever is being hurt and nobody to tell. Nobody to support you. Being alone in your hangups, depression and fears. I'm 72 and have evolved into an old lady who has no filter. No patience. No tolerance for phonies and liars. The worst thing anyone can do to me is lie to me. It turns me right off. I'm not a bitter old lady. Just an old lady that don't take no shit. There is no woman or anyone for that matter that can find all the pieces after childhood rape. No one. I am writing about a child from long ago. These writings were written many years ago. Saved them for this, and hopefully these words will help troubled souls find some way to have a positive life without the missing pieces that are forever gone. These last words are here to help women and girls find something in themselves to love. Not approval from other people.

I'm a hermit and loner. Yes, this is true. I spent most of my life alone. Even now I'm alone and it does get to me sometimes. If it's meant to be I will find friends that can appreciate me and my complex mind. I'm brutally honest. I have to hold back most of the time. My life, or should I say what's left of it is ok. It can always be worse. We have to train our minds to appreciate what we have. I hope that being for real, always searching the reasons why I have evolved into this complex woman. I realize that this is me. I will not even try to change one thing about me. I love myself. Unbelievably so and hope other girls and women with low self-esteem and broken hearts will learn to do the same. Those missing pieces that I tried to find will unfortunately be lost forever. They are not recognizable anymore. I don't need them. I have figured out how to love and appreciate what is left of me. I hope this book has helped someone find the reason to love again.

So, these last few words in this book will close this chapter in my life. To all the young girl and women that have lost their selves and love and appreciation of who they have become. The leftovers of abuse and self-abuse. I hope these words find their way to all the fractured souls trying to find the broken pieces. Love you all, be strong and stay strong.

Darlene Olaiya

The Completion of the Long and Painful Journey of Healing

This book was written to heal my soul. It is about the reason why I am still here. The thousands of girls and women that have survived horrendous experiences and need encouragement to move forward in a positive way. It shows the fractured souls a way to break free from self-abuse. It took two years to stop abusing myself. To forgive myself.

Years to find a reason to love myself. I spent over 25 years recovering from horrible experiences that I had created and wasn't able to solve the problem. The escape from myself, my self-made prison was so difficult. This book hopefully is going to show these tortured souls how to escape. How to find the reason to even try to move forward in a positive way. These are the closing thoughts and along with them the answer to the hopelessness of a life that has been heartbreaking with no way out. I hope and pray that these words are going to show the tortured souls how to love themselves. This is the only way out. Self-love, self-appreciation. Self-respect. GOD BLESS